D1499653

DISCARD

MAYFLOWER

Rebecca Siegel

Michael Lauritano & Mike Love

words & pictures

Quarto is the authority on a wide range of topics.

Quarto educates, entertains and enriches the lives of our readers—enthusiasts and lovers of hands-on living.

www.quartoknows.com

Author: Rebecca Siegel
Illustrators: Michael Lauritano and Mike Love
Maritime History Consultant: Michael P. Dyer
Native Peoples Consultant: Chief George Spring Buffalo
Designer: Karen Hood
Editor: Harriet Stone
Editorial Director: Laura Knowles
Art Director: Susi Martin
Creative Director: Malena Stojic
Group Publisher: Maxime Boucknooghe

First published in 2020 by words & pictures,
an imprint of The Quarto Group.
26391 Crown Valley Parkway, Suite 220
Mission Viejo, CA 92691, USA
T: +1 949 380 7510
F: +1 949 380 7575
www.QuartoKnows.com

A CIP record for this book is available from the
Library of Congress.

ISBN: 978 0 7112 4825 0

Manufactured in Guangzhou, China EB052020

9 8 7 6 5 4 3 2 1

MIX
Paper from
responsible sources
FSC® C124385
www.fsc.org

THE MAYFLOWER

In the fall of 1620, a small wooden ship bobbed in a harbor in Plymouth, England. Crammed below deck were about 100 passengers. They were preparing to sail to America to start a new life. This journey typically took about two months and was often dangerous and difficult.

The passengers didn't know it, but they would do much more than just survive their voyage. They would take the first steps toward founding a nation.

Across the sea, vast networks of Native People farmed, hunted, and thrived. They, too, were unaware that their lives were about to change forever. A little ship called the *Mayflower* was setting sail.

CONTENTS

RELIGIOUS FREEDOM

What caused these people to leave England in search of a new homeland? In the years leading up to the *Mayflower's* voyage, religious life in England had changed drastically. The national church, called the Church of England, was Protestant, but it still had some Catholic traits. Some Protestants did not like this. They thought that removing Catholic practices from their church would help it become pure. They became known as Puritans.

THE SAINTS

Some Puritans tried to distance themselves from the Church of England. They withdrew from their community churches to form small congregations in their homes or local meeting places. As time went on, some of them looked for a way to fully separate themselves from the Church of England. These Puritans called themselves "Saints." To the general public, they became known as separatists.

AGAINST THE LAW

The King did not support the separatists. He wanted his people to unite under the Church of England. People were required to attend church and it became illegal to hold private religious meetings. This meant that the separatist meetings were against the law.

One group of separatists in Scrooby, Nottinghamshire decided to flee England. They hoped to find religious freedom in another country. However, leaving England without permission from the King was illegal, so they tried to sneak out. At first, some were caught and jailed, but later the group made it to Leiden, Holland and established their own church there.

"I shall make them conform, else I shall harry them out of this land, or even worse."

KING JAMES, 1604

LEIDEN, HOLLAND

Life in Holland was not perfect for the separatists. The Dutch culture felt very different from their English roots. They had to work long, hard hours in Holland's booming cloth trade. They also feared that the Dutch would soon be at war with Spain. If that happened and Spain won, then their new home would be under Catholic rule.

Something became clear to the Saints: they needed a new place to build their church.

LEAVING HOLLAND

Tales from America had been trickling back to Europe for more than 100 years. The Spanish, Dutch, and French had already explored some of its vast lands. Their reports were promising: America was a wild, sprawling, beautiful place. In 1607, just 13 years before the *Mayflower* would set sail, an Englishman named Captain John Smith helped to set up a colony in Jamestown, Virginia.

BIG PLANS

The Leiden separatists began planning their own move to Virginia. They got a document from the Virginia Company which gave them permission to form a colony near the Hudson River. They also got support from businessmen who hoped to make money from American goods. To make the trip across the ocean, the Leiden separatists bought a small ship called the *Speedwell*. Then they asked businessmen in London to find them a second ship.

THE *SPEEDWELL*

In July 1620, the Leiden group traveled to Delfshaven, Holland, where the first brave travelers boarded the *Speedwell*. It was a tearful farewell. The group did not know if they would ever see one another again. On July 22, the *Speedwell* set sail for England to pick up more passengers and meet up with its companion vessel, a ship called the *Mayflower*.

"It was a sad and mournful parting...
to see what sighs and sobs did
sound amongst them, what tears
did gush from every eye."

MAYFLOWER PASSENGER, WILLIAM BRADFORD

ABOUT THE MAYFLOWER

The boxy ship awaiting the Leiden group in Southampton was not an impressive craft. Though bigger than the *Speedwell*, the *Mayflower* was still quite small. Measured from stern to bow, she was only about 100 feet long. She was also old. Her wooden hull was worn and tired. She had sailed for more than 10 years and was near the end of such a ship's career.

ARMED WITH GUNS

The *Mayflower* was a merchant ship. This meant that she was built to carry goods, such as cloth or wine. Merchant ships were sometimes attacked or captured by military ships from other countries. Because of this, ships like the *Mayflower* were heavily armed. Gunports dotted the *Mayflower*'s sides. If she was ever attacked, her crew could open these hatches and slide out the cannons—and there were plenty of cannons to use! The *Mayflower* carried about seven large cannons that could fire long distances, and three smaller guns.

THE SPEEDWELL

THE MAYFLOWER

AN UNCOMFORTABLE SHIP

Even from the outside, the *Mayflower* looked
uncomfortable. There weren't many windows
as they would let seawater in during storms.
The small deck didn't have space to sit or rest
—in fact, it didn't have any furniture at all.
This was not going to be a relaxing journey;
it was going to be very difficult, indeed.

Adding to the Saints' discomfort was the fact that
they would not be the only passengers on this voyage.
The London businessmen had decided to send a group
of their own people along for the trip as well. Many of
these people were Puritans, but none were part of the
Leiden separatists. Though they would soon come to
know one another very well, the Leiden group gave
their shipmates a name that reflected how they felt
about outsiders. They called them "Strangers."

INSIDE THE SHIP

The *Mayflower*'s interior was filled with supplies, nautical tools, food, drink, and weapons. Each room served its own purpose.

KEY:

1 **POOP HOUSE:** This is where Captain Christopher Jones used navigational tools to direct the *Mayflower* toward America.

2 **CABIN:** This is where Master Jones slept.

3 **FORECASTLE:** Most of the ship's crew slept here. It is also where meals would have been cooked.

4 **LONGBOAT:** A small craft used to sail between the *Mayflower* and the shore.

5 **STEERAGE ROOM:** This room held the whip-staff, a tool used to move the ship's rudder, which steered the *Mayflower*. The ship's officers also likely slept here.

6 **GUN ROOM:** The ammunition and gunpowder were stored here.

7 **GUN DECK:** This area housed the ship's cannons. It is also where most of the passengers stayed.

8 **CARGO HOLD:** This is where the passengers' belongings and supplies were stored. On other missions, this is where cargo such as wine would have been kept.

SETTING SAIL

As their departure approached, the Saints and Strangers boarded their boats. Their journey was about to unite them under a single title: Pilgrims.

TROUBLE WITH THE *SPEEDWELL*

On August 5, 1620, the two ships set sail for America. They did not get far. The *Speedwell* began leaking. Both ships stopped at the town of Dartmouth while the *Speedwell* was repaired. On August 21, the boats raised their sails for America. They had only traveled about 300 miles out to sea when the *Speedwell's* problems returned. Both ships turned around and harbored in Plymouth, England. There, it was decided that the *Speedwell* could not make the journey.

The passengers on the two ships faced a decision. They could abandon their quest, or they could pile into the remaining ship and continue on. Some people, spooked or simply tired of the delays, took their things and went back home. Others remained committed to their journey. They moved the important supplies from the *Speedwell* into the *Mayflower*, then crowded together below decks.

THE *MAYFLOWER* SETS SAIL

On September 6, the *Mayflower's* crew steered her out of Plymouth Harbor. They unfurled her huge, canvas sails and secured them with sturdy rope. Soon, the wind caught the sails and sent the *Mayflower* darting across the waves. The journey had finally begun.

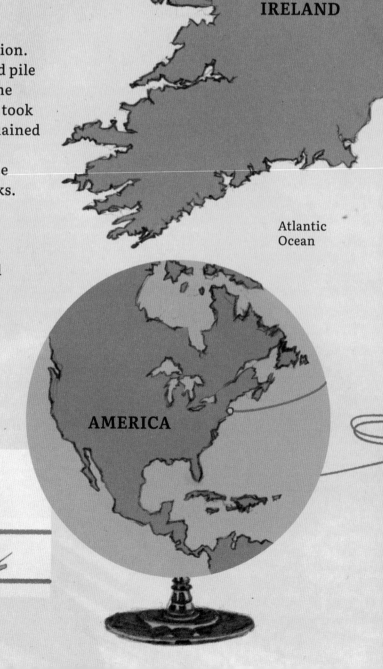

IRELAND

Atlantic Ocean

AMERICA

MAYFLOWER

SPEEDWELL

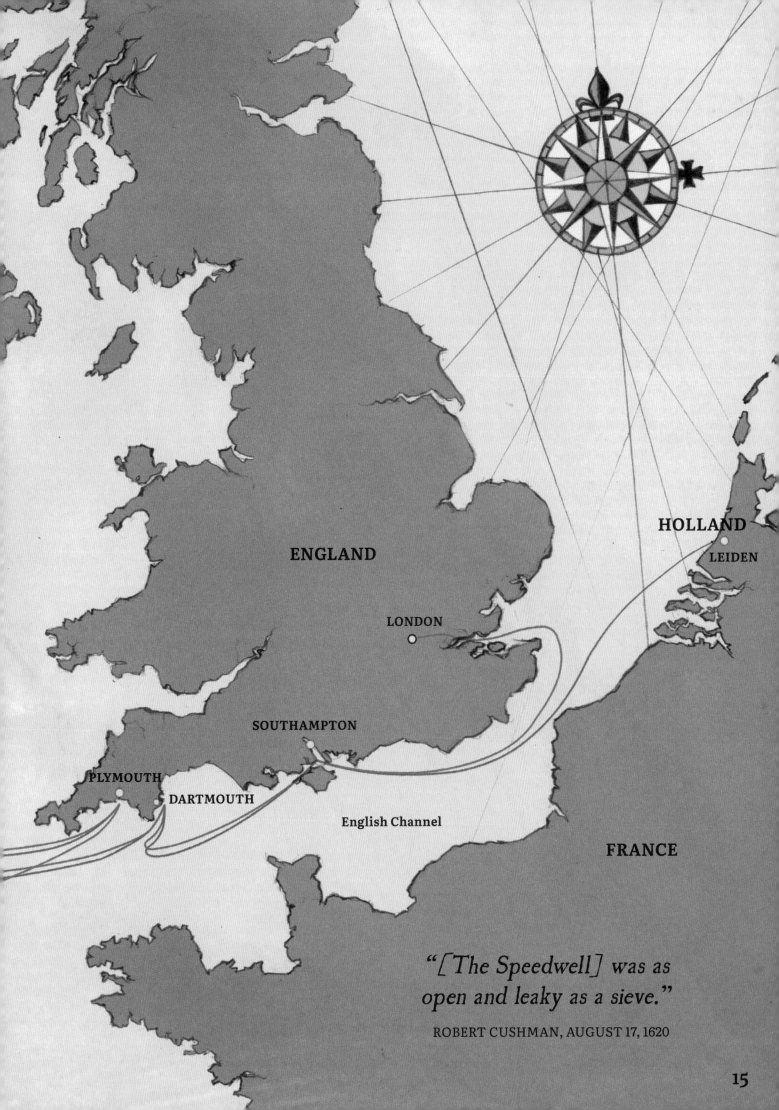

SCOTLAND

ENGLAND

LONDON

HOLLAND

LEIDEN

SOUTHAMPTON

PLYMOUTH

DARTMOUTH

English Channel

FRANCE

"[The Speedwell] was as
open and leaky as a sieve."

ROBERT CUSHMAN, AUGUST 17, 1620

15

SHIPMATES

There were about 24 family groups crammed onto the *Mayflower*.
Fifteen families were Saints from the Leiden group. The remaining nine
households were the Strangers. Some of the Strangers were people
traveling to America for financial reasons. Others had been hired by the
Virginia Company to help grow the population of the new settlement.
Among the passengers were:

SAINTS

JOHN AND CATHERINE CARVER
This couple was very wealthy.
John was a leader in the church
and community.

WILLIAM AND MARY BREWSTER
William was a religious leader
within the Leiden group. They
traveled with their children who
were named Love and Wrestling.

**WILLIAM AND
DOROTHY BRADFORD**
William was an organizer of the
trip to America. The Bradfords
left their young son behind
with family in Leiden.

> *"It is not with us as with other men, whom small things can discourage, or small discontentments cause to wish themselves at home again."*
>
> PASSENGER WILLIAM BREWSTER AND
> LEIDEN CHURCH PASTOR, JOHN ROBINSON, 1617

STRANGERS

MYLES AND ROSE STANDISH
Myles was a soldier. He was sent to help protect the settlement from the Native People living there.

STEVEN AND ELIZABETH HOPKINS
Steven had been to the New World before and had experience with Native People. Elizabeth was pregnant. The Hopkins traveled with two servants and their children, Constance, Giles, and Damaris.

ELLEN, JASPER, MARY, AND RICHARD MORE
The More children were on the *Mayflower* without their parents, who had recently divorced. Their father sent them to America in the hope that they could have a fresh start there.

SERVANTS
About a fifth of the passengers on the *Mayflower* were servants.

HUMILITY COOPER
Humility was the *Mayflower*'s youngest passenger. She was just one year old.

PACKING FOR A NEW LIFE

The Pilgrims would find no stores or hotels awaiting them in America. This meant that they had to pack carefully. They brought the supplies they needed to survive the voyage across the sea. They also packed the tools necessary to build a community once they arrived in Virginia.

Settlers who had traveled to New England sometimes sent home lists of supplies they recommended for future travelers. These lists suggest what a couple traveling on the *Mayflower* might have packed to help them survive the journey or the first years in New England.

FOOD AND DRINK

16 barrels of ground meal

4 hogsheads of beer

2 hogsheads of vinegar

4 bushels of peas

4 bushels of oatmeal

2 bushels of mustard seeds

2 gallons of oil

224 pounds of fish

2 gallons of liquor

CLOTHING

1 stocking cap

1 hat

1 waistcoat

3 pairs of stockings

3 shirts

4 pairs of shoes

3 suits

2 bodices

3 bonnets

1 shawl

2 skirts

2 aprons

HOUSEHOLD ITEMS

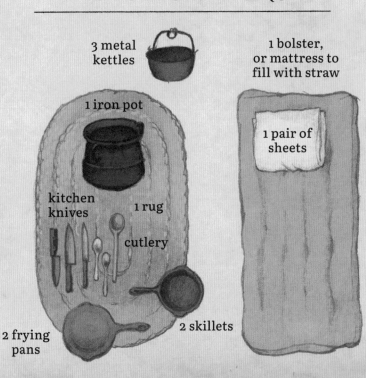

3 metal kettles

1 bolster, or mattress to fill with straw

1 iron pot

1 pair of sheets

kitchen knives

1 rug

cutlery

2 frying pans

2 skillets

WOODWORKING AND LABOR TOOLS FOR A FAMILY

3 saws

2 pick axes

2 spades

9 axes and hatchets

10 hoes

3 shovels

6 chisels

nails

WEAPONS

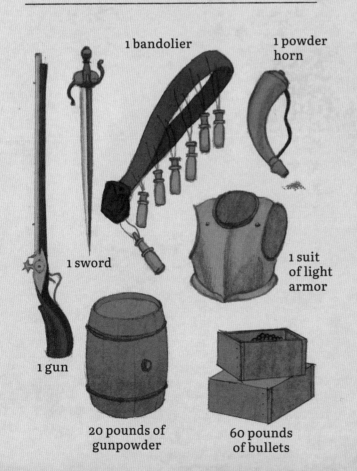

1 bandolier

1 powder horn

1 sword

1 suit of light armor

1 gun

20 pounds of gunpowder

60 pounds of bullets

EXTRA ITEMS

Some families managed to bring a few extra treasured items with them. Select pieces of furniture, such as wooden chests, made the trip. Susanna White was pregnant when she boarded the *Mayflower* so she and her husband brought a wicker baby cradle along for the journey.

The Leiden Pilgrims also brought a tool they called a "great iron screw." This was likely a building tool that helped lift or hold large items. They could use it to erect their homes in New England.

FURRY COMPANIONS

Passenger John Goodman brought two furry items along for the trip: his dogs. One was a spaniel, the other was an English mastiff. They would be used to help hunt for deer and birds.

THE CREW

There were between 25 and 30 crewmembers on the *Mayflower*. They slept in shifts in the forecastle. Doing this kept the boat properly crewed at all times, and made their cramped quarters a little more comfortable.

MASTER AND MATES

The ship's master, or captain, Christopher Jones was about 50 years old and an experienced leader and seaman, though this would be his first trip to America. Two master's mates, Robert Crippen and John Clarke, helped Jones to inspect the ship and maintain order during the journey. Clarke likely worked as the ship's pilot keeping her on course. Both mates had been to New England on previous journeys.

BOATSWAIN

He was in charge of maintaining the *Mayflower's* rigging, sails, and anchors.

SWABBER

The crew took turns with this role because it was particularly foul. The swabber and an assistant were in charge of scrubbing the decks.

CARPENTER

He worked hard to keep the *Mayflower's* hull strong and free from leaks.

SHIP'S SURGEON

This was a man named Giles Heale. His job on the journey was to help passengers who were injured or became ill from sicknesses such as cholera, dysentery, or scurvy. Heale was not very experienced. It is likely that this was his first major journey.

COOK

This man prepared meals and managed food stores. He probably worked in the forecastle.

MASTER GUNNER

He was responsible for maintaining the ship's store of weapons and ammunition. If the *Mayflower* was attacked, his job would be crucial.

QUARTERMASTERS

These men took care of the ship's cargo. They also maintained the ship's lines and fishing equipment.

COOPER

This was a man named John Alden. He worked to build and repair wooden barrels on board the ship. This was a crucial job since all of the ship's food and drink was stored in barrels.

VIOLENT SEAS

To the south of the *Mayflower*'s route, groups of thieving sailors terrorized the seas: pirates! These cunning seamen searched the horizon for cargo ships such as the *Mayflower*, and then attacked.

Sometimes, pirate attacks were relatively peaceful. Merchant ships could simply surrender themselves, allowing pirates to come on board and take what they wanted. Other times, they were brutal affairs. Pirates would kill the crew and passengers on their target ships, sometimes by tossing them overboard. Pirates occasionally captured a ship's crew and sold them into slavery.

The *Mayflower*'s passengers slept in the gun deck, amid the ship's collection of cannons. These weapons would have helped defend the ship if the need arose. Luckily, they did not face any pirates on their voyage.

*"As in all lands where there are many people,
there are some thieves, so in all seas
much frequented, there are some pirates."*

CAPTAIN JOHN SMITH

NAVIGATING THE SEAS

The vast blue ocean stretched out on all sides of the *Mayflower*. White clouds dotted the sky. The ship's crew knew their destination: Virginia. However, they had few tools to help them find the way there.

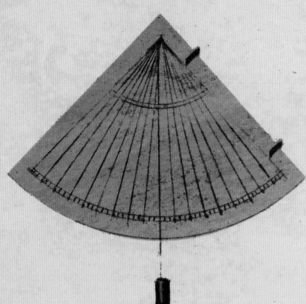

QUADRANT

Sailors used this tool to measure their latitude (how far north or south they were). They peered at the North Star along one of the quadrant's straight edges, and then recorded the point where a weighted string hung along the quadrant's scale, which was carved into its curved edge. This measurement helped them find their latitude.

CROSS-STAFF

Sailors could also find their latitude by measuring the height of the Pole Star above their ship. To do this they used a tool called a cross-staff.

SANDGLASS

These fragile tools helped sailors measure time. Many ships carried sandglasses in different sizes to measure different times, such as one hour, half hour, and half a minute.

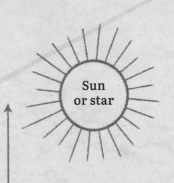

Sun
or star

Horizon

COMPASS ROSE

These 32-point stars allowed sailors
to precisely work out their direction.

RUDDER

The *Mayflower* did not have a steering wheel.
Instead, she used her rudder to change direction.
On the *Mayflower*, this job was managed by John
Clark, the ship's pilot. Clark could not actually see
where the ship was going from his place in the
Steerage Room, so other crew members shouted
instructions down to him through an open hatch.

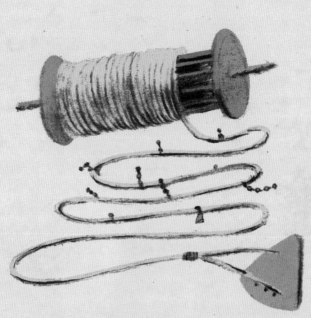

LOG LINE

This device helped to work out the
speed a ship was going. It was a flat,
heavy piece of wood attached to a
coiled rope. The rope had bits of fabric
or twine knotted to it at set distances.
Sailors would throw the piece of wood
overboard and count the number of
knots that unwound from the spool
in a set amount of time. A ship's speed
is still measured in knots today.

LIFE AT SEA

Above decks, the *Mayflower* was a bright, noisy place. Crisp blue water lapped at the ship's hull. Thick oak boards creaked and groaned. White sails stretched in the wind. Rowdy crewmembers shouted and joked with one another in the sunshine.

A FOUL PLACE

Down in the gun deck, murmured conversations filled the dark, dank air. Rough dividers made of sheets or stacked belongings made the already-cramped area seem even smaller. Though the passengers worked hard to keep their area clean, their quarters would have smelled foul. No one could bathe while on the journey, so the odor of sweat hung in the air. Mold, too, tainted their living space, and water had soaked many of their belongings.

COOKING

Cooking at sea was a difficult task and could be dangerous. An open flame might ignite the wooden ship, so most of the meals eaten on the *Mayflower* would have been cold. Items like biscuits, dried meat, and pickled foods were served. Everyone on the ship, including children, drank "small beer"—a low-alcohol drink.

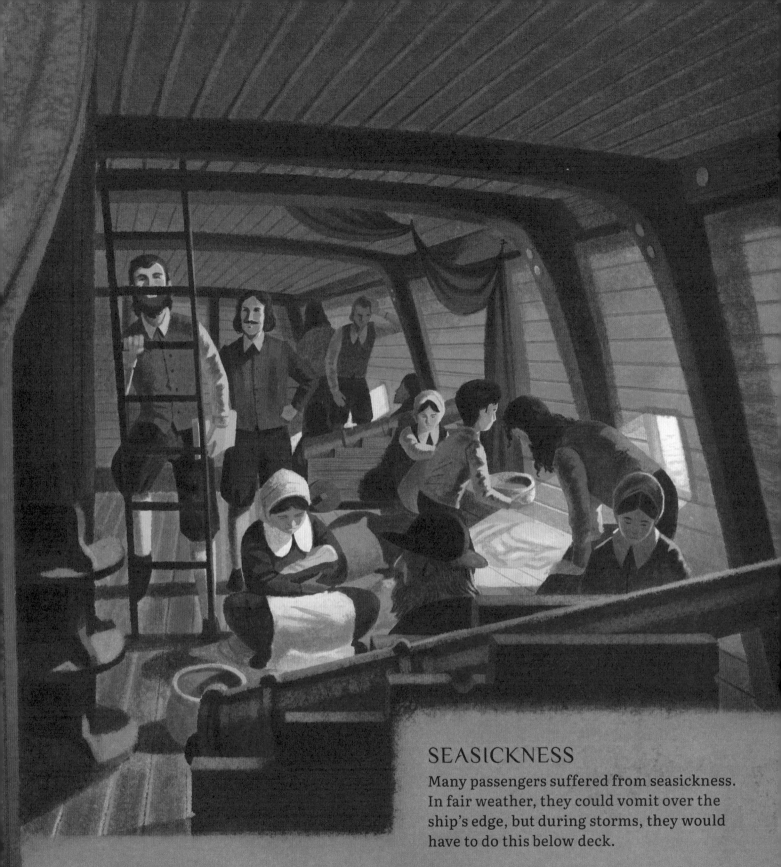

CHAMBER POTS

The *Mayflower* did not have any bathrooms. Passengers used chamber pots and emptied them into the sea. This became problematic in storms, when people had to stay below deck. They could not empty their chamber pots, which sloshed around on the rough sea's waves. Spilled chamber pots made the boat dirty and smelly.

SEASICKNESS

Many passengers suffered from seasickness. In fair weather, they could vomit over the ship's edge, but during storms, they would have to do this below deck.

As summer turned to fall, life on the *Mayflower* became more unpleasant. The Pilgrims grew cold. Their damp clothes clung to their shivering frames. Despite the wet and foul conditions, the *Mayflower* passengers kept in good spirits. They were eager to start their new lives in Virginia. Then, about halfway across the Atlantic, the skies grew dark.

STORMS

About 1,500 miles from England, storm clouds gathered in the sky. Wind lashed the ship and giant waves crashed against her hull. She pitched and rocked. Water leaked between the thick, oak boards. The passengers huddled in the gun deck felt afraid. Then, things got worse. The howling winds grew stronger, causing a large beam supporting the main deck to bend. Then it cracked.

FEAR

The crew was scared. They argued with one another about what to do. Should they abandon their mission, or should they press on? Captain Christopher Jones settled the argument. They would continue on, he declared, but first they had to fix the broken beam.

Jones ordered the Pilgrims to retrieve the "great iron screw" brought for homebuilding in New England. They used the screw to lift the giant beam back into place. Then, the ship's carpenter secured it. The crew got to work fixing the ship's many leaks, filling gaps in the old timber with gluey caulk. Slowly, the leaking lessened. The *Mayflower* was once again seaworthy.

HOPING TO SURVIVE

Crushing swells continued to rock the ship violently. The winds grew so fierce that the crew feared her masts would snap. If this happened, they would be stranded at sea. Crew members braved the decks and pulled down the giant canvas sails. They hoped this might help the ship survive. However, without her sails, the *Mayflower* couldn't continue on her journey toward America. Instead she bobbed in place, waiting for the storm to pass. No one knew how long this would take. If they spent too long at sea, the passengers would run out of food and drink, and wouldn't last much longer.

Yet still, the storms raged on.

SAVED AND LOST

Giant waves continued to toss the *Mayflower* back and forth. The passengers cowered in the gun deck. Vomit, spilled chamber pots, and old food polluted the dark hold, but the passengers took comfort there all the same. At least the shelter kept them safe from the lashing waves and wind.

JOHN HOWLAND

During the storm, 21-year-old John Howland decided to leave the gun deck. He climbed the steep ladder and ventured into the open air. Howland was on the trip as a servant to the wealthy Leiden Pilgrim, John Carver. William Bradford described Howland as a "lusty young man." This suggests that Bradford thought Howland was too wild or behaved inappropriately. As he ventured out onto the deck mid-storm, Howland's behavior was certainly reckless.

Soon, a wave slammed the ship. The deck pitched to the side and Howland was swept into the water. As he fell, he caught a rope that was dangling overboard and clung to it fiercely. The water was icy and rough. People rushed to his aid. Someone held out a long tool called a boathook, using it to snag Howland and pull him in. Finally, Howland was heaved back onto the deck, cold and shaken, but alive.

LOST

Not everyone shared Howland's luck. Two people died during the
Mayflower's journey. One was a young servant named William Butten,
who was only about 15 years old. The other was a member of the crew who
had been cruel to the Leiden Puritans. He had made fun of their seasickness,
and even said that he "hoped to cast half of them overboard" before the
end of their trip. William Bradford later wrote that this sailor's "curses"
fell "on his own head." He died of a disease about
halfway across the ocean, and his body
was dumped overboard.

LANDING IN THE NEW WORLD

On the morning of November 9, 1620, the *Mayflower's* weary crew spotted something in the distance. It was a strip of land. Blue-green trees hugged a curved shoreline. They were looking at Cape Cod, a place almost 250 miles north of their intended destination of Virginia. When the Saints saw the land ahead, they dropped to their knees and thanked God.

MORE STORMS

Master Jones commanded the ship southeast, toward Virginia. However, he was soon met by another storm. Huge waves and heavy winds pounded the *Mayflower*. The little ship could not safely continue on. Jones turned north and made for a small, protected area called Cape Cod Bay. On November 11, the crew dropped anchor in what is now called Provincetown Harbor.

A HOPEFUL PLACE

The passengers gazed at their new surroundings with hope. Tall, healthy trees sprung from the sandy shores. Water fowl dotted the skies. It looked like a fertile, welcoming place. Some of the exhausted travelers started dreaming of a busy future for the little bay. One later wrote, hopefully, that "it is a harbor wherein a thousand sail of ships may safely ride."

All around the *Mayflower*, large black whales frolicked in the water. The passengers watched them with delight and awe. It was a powerful sight. They had arrived in a new and very different world.

*"...we espied land which was deemed to be Cape Cod...
And the appearance of it much comforted us, especially seeing
so goodly a land, and wooded to the brink of the sea."*

WILLIAM BRADFORD

HUNGER AND SICKNESS
Everyone on the *Mayflower* was hungry and
tired. They searched the waters for cod or
other fish to eat, managing to catch a few
small fish, but it was not enough for them.
Some collected mussels, but these made them
ill. They would soon need to leave the boat
in search of fresh food, wood, and water.

THE MAYFLOWER COMPACT

Tensions on the ship ran high. After more than two months crammed together, many of the passengers were not getting along. Some of the Strangers' behavior upset the Saints. They worried about what might happen when everyone went ashore. The area of Cape Cod was not included in their document from the Virginia Company. This meant that they were outside of the company's rule. They were on their own.

The Saints wanted to do something to protect themselves from lawlessness, so they wrote a document known as a "compact," to create a temporary government. This would maintain order until they could get a new document from England allowing them to stay where they had landed. It would also keep their little group united in the days and months to come.

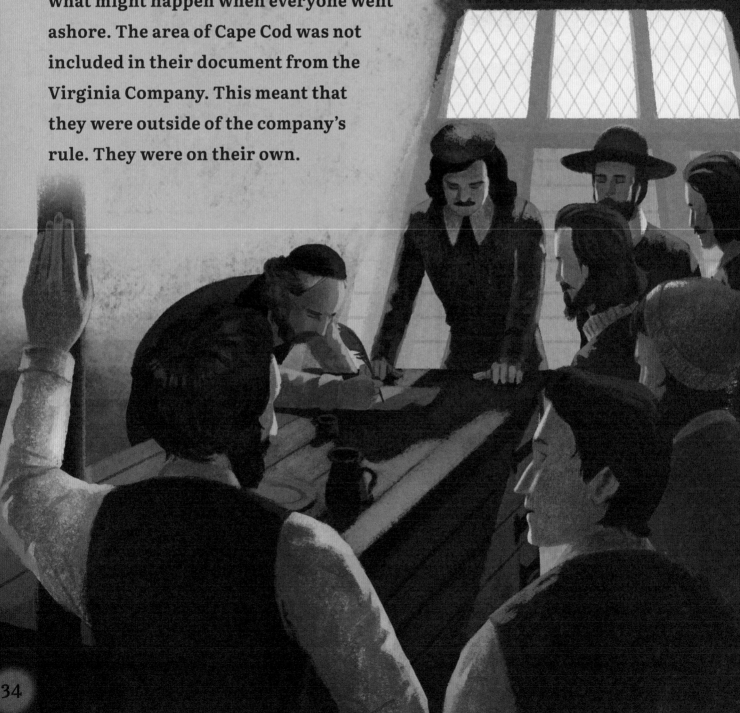

WRITING A COMPACT

Finally, one of the Leiden Pilgrims sat down with a quill and paper. He began writing: "In the name of God, Amen...

...Having undertaken, for the glory of God, and advancement of the Christian faith, and honor of our king and country, a voyage to plant the first colony in the northern parts of Virginia, do by these presents solemnly and mutually in the presence of God and one of another, covenant, and combine ourselves together into a civil body politic, for our better ordering and preservation, and furtherance of the ends aforesaid; and by virtue hereof to enact, constitute, and frame such just and equal laws, ordinances, acts, constitutions, offices from time to time, as shall be thought most meet and convenient for the general good of the colony: unto which we promise all due submission and obedience...

This would later become known as the Mayflower Compact. At the bottom of the document, 41 adult male passengers added their names. Women were not invited to sign, nor were they part of the discussion about law and order in the New World. This was typical for the time and culture.

THE NATIVE PEOPLE

The *Mayflower* had not arrived in an empty land. Native People lived throughout North America. Just off of Cape Cod lived a large nation called the Wampanoag. There were approximately 40,000 Wampanoag people living in 67 settlements in New England in the early 1600s. In fact, some earlier explorers abandoned the idea of settling in Cape Cod because the area was too crowded with people. Early European explorers noted that these people were healthy and strong.

FLOURISHING CULTURE

The Wampanoag were excellent hunters, farmers, and fishers. Early European visitors described seeing the Wampanoag's flourishing farms, orchards, and gardens. After living on the land for approximately 10,000 years, these people clearly knew how to thrive on it.

There were other Native tribes in New England, each with its own identity and politics. A large trade network existed between tribes. When Europeans arrived in North America, they entered into that network, trading items such as glass, metal, and cloth. In return, they received food, animal skins, or other goods.

DANGEROUS INTERACTIONS

Interacting with Europeans could be very dangerous. They were known to kidnap Native People and sell them as slaves. Occasionally, the Europeans and Native People engaged in bloody fights, but the greatest threat came from disease. Europeans carried illnesses that the Native People had no immunity to.

KIDNAPPED

Six years before the *Mayflower* set sail, a group of English sailors had arrived at a Cape Cod Wampanoag village called Patuxet. They were there to fish and hunt for whale, but one Englishman wanted something else as well. He kidnapped a group of Wampanoag people and took them to Europe to sell as slaves. The Wampanoag were furious.

"*as beautiful of stature and build as I can possibly describe.*"

GIOVANNI DA VERRAZZANO, EUROPEAN EXPLORER
DESCRIBING THE NATIVE PEOPLE, 1524

THE GREAT DYING

Because of the kidnappings, two years later when French sailors were wrecked on their shores, the Wampanoag attacked and took some men prisoner. The prisoners likely infected the Wampanoag with a deadly disease. By the time the *Mayflower* arrived, about 90 percent of the Native People in coastal New England had died. The Wampanoag called this the Great Dying.

"A WONDERFUL PLAGUE"

When King James I learned of the terrible diseases in North America, he said "this wonderful plague among the savages" showed that God wanted the land there to be "possessed and enjoyed" by the English. The King's words showed that the English did not feel sympathy for the Native People's struggles. Instead, they wanted the tribes out of the way.

EXPLORING

The Pilgrims felt a chill in the air. Back in England,
the fall weather had been pleasant. Now, in Cape Cod Bay,
the wind was cold and biting. Winter was approaching.
It was time to leave the safe haven of the boat.

SETTING OFF

Four days after dropping anchor, a group
of men boarded the ship's longboat and set
off toward land. The explorers were looking
for fresh water and a good site for their
settlement, but they were ready for
something else: a fight. Tales of America's
Native People had reached them back in
Europe. They heard that these were evil,
unsophisticated people. Some might
have even believed that the Native People
would kill and eat them.

The Pilgrims were dressed for battle.
They wore metal armor and carried guns
and swords. As their longboat pulled ashore,
they looked for signs of Native People.
They stepped onto the sandy beach and
cautiously set off into the new land. Soon,
they spotted a group of five or six Native
People. The Pilgrims hurried toward them.

WEAK AND TIRED

Spotting the Pilgrims, the Native People swiftly fled into the thickets. The Pilgrims were too weighed down by bulky armor and heavy weapons to keep up and soon lost sight of the Native People. They trudged on until nightfall. Hungry and thirsty, the Pilgrims made camp and collapsed. The next morning, the men marched on. By now, they were ragged. They had only brought a small bottle of liquor to drink and some hard bread and cheese to eat. They needed nourishment.

Midmorning, the Pilgrims walked into a deep valley, teeming with wildlife. Tall grass and scrub hugged the ground. A deer wandered past. Fresh water trickled from springs. The men fell onto the water and drank eagerly.

TRADE

Though the Pilgrims were wary of the Native People, they also wanted to meet them. They hoped to trade with them for things like seeds, food, and beaver skins. Beaver was very valuable in Europe, as beaver felt hats were popular and expensive. If the Pilgrims could send back enough beaver skins, they could earn money to help them repay the businessmen in London who had funded their trip.

"We drunk our first New England water with as much delight as we ever drunk drink in all our lives."

EDWARD WINSLOW

FIRST THEFTS

As the explorers wandered on, they found clues that Native People had tended this land. Near a clear, blue pond was an abandoned corn field. A little path led to strange mounds of sand. The Pilgrims did not know what the mounds held or what they meant, so they decided to investigate.

The Pilgrims dug into one mound and found a bow and arrow. Wondering if it was a grave, they quickly returned the items and tried to make it look as though they had not touched the mound. They walked on and soon found more old corn fields and an abandoned dwelling. Nearby was another mound that looked new. They dug into it and found corn seed and a bushel of corn still on the cob.

The Pilgrims had never seen this type of corn before. Some of the ears were a vivid red or yellow, while others were a mix of beautiful blues.

The Pilgrims argued about what to do. They were hungry and weak. The ears could feed them and the seed could help them survive, but this corn belonged to the Native People. Already, they had dug up a grave. Were they going to steal the corn, too? A ring of men stood guard around the discussion. They watched for Native People. Finally, the Pilgrims made a decision: they would take the fresh corn and as much of the seed as they could hold. Later, they would repay the Native People. They returned to their ship with their loot.

MORE CORN

November marched on and the temperatures dropped. The Pilgrims returned to the mounds and took more corn. Nearby they found more buried supplies: wheat, beans, and oil, which they quickly took for themselves. The Pilgrims also found two Native homes. They ducked inside and found tools, dishes, seeds, and plenty of dried food. They pocketed the best items.

Again, the Pilgrims discussed leaving something for the Native People as payment, but they had forgotten to bring anything with them. They decided to wait until later when they could "meet conveniently with them." This would not happen for another six months. By that time, their thefts had led to much anger with the Native People.

THE "PRETTIEST THINGS"

On their way back to the *Mayflower*, the Pilgrims found another grave. They dug it up and found the bodies of an adult man and a child inside. The man had yellow hair, so the Pilgrims wondered if he was European. Both bodies were buried with many beautiful items. The Pilgrims collected the "prettiest things" from the grave, and left.

These thefts show that the Pilgrims did not think of the Native People as their equals. The Wampanoag buried important items with their loved ones so that they might take them into the afterworld. Anyone who would steal those items did not respect their culture or traditions.

THE FIRST ENCOUNTER

On the *Mayflower*, passengers were cold and cramped. Despite the poor conditions on board, in late November, Susanna White birthed a baby boy she named Peregrine, meaning "one who journeys to foreign lands." Another child had been born during the ship's journey. He was named Oceanus.

The Pilgrims were ready to journey ashore again. They were tired of being on the harbored ship. On December 6, 1620, a group of men boarded the ship's longboat and set off for land.

The icy temperatures made the trip from the *Mayflower* to the sandy shore miserable. Their wet clothing froze solid. The next two nights, the Pilgrims camped around a fire and slept uneasily. Sounds in the forest made them jump. They were afraid that the Native People would attack them.

"They are men! Indians! Indians!"

"INDIANS!"

Early the morning of December 8, 1620, the Pilgrims ate breakfast and prayed. A few members of the group went down to the beach to prepare their longboat. The rest stayed around the camp. Suddenly, a strange cry rang out. One of the Pilgrims came running into the camp, shouting. Arrows began slicing through the air. The Pilgrims scrambled to their big, bulky guns. Myles Standish fired a shot. Others heaved their huge weapons into place and fired.

The fight was slow and in close quarters. It took time for the Pilgrims to aim their heavy weapons. The Native People had crept close enough to their camp to see their targets clearly, but this meant that they were within firing range. For a while, the air was filled with musket shot and razor-sharp arrows. Then, with a great shout, the Native People retreated. The fight was over. No one had died.

The Pilgrims later named this area after the battle. They called it First Encounter Beach.

NEW PLYMOUTH

The Pilgrims did not want the *Mayflower* to remain where it was, harbored in Cape Cod Bay. They hoped to move closer to the area they would permanently settle. On December 15, the *Mayflower* raised its anchor and sailed toward a place called New Plymouth.

PLYMOUTH ROCK
The *Mayflower* laid anchor near what is now known as Plymouth Rock. Whether the Pilgrims stepped onto it as they walked ashore is not known. The legend surrounding the rock was first recorded much later.

The Pilgrims decided to make New Plymouth their new home. Edward Winslow wrote that it was "on a high ground, where there is a great deal of land cleared, and hath been planted with corn three or four years ago" with "many delicate springs of good water as can be drunk."

A LONG WINTER

As the *Mayflower* bobbed peacefully just off New Plymouth, a terrible sickness began to sweep through her gun deck. This dark and foul space filled with coughs, moans, and sighs—and then the dying began. Each day, someone died. Sometimes, as many as two or three were lost in a day. The illness almost destroyed the entire group. There were times when only six or seven Pilgrims were healthy enough to help the others.

The strongest of the group continued to go onto land. They hunted for wild animals to bring back to the ship. They also worked on some of the first buildings for their settlement, but progress was slow. They were frail, and tired, and spent much of their energy burying their dead.

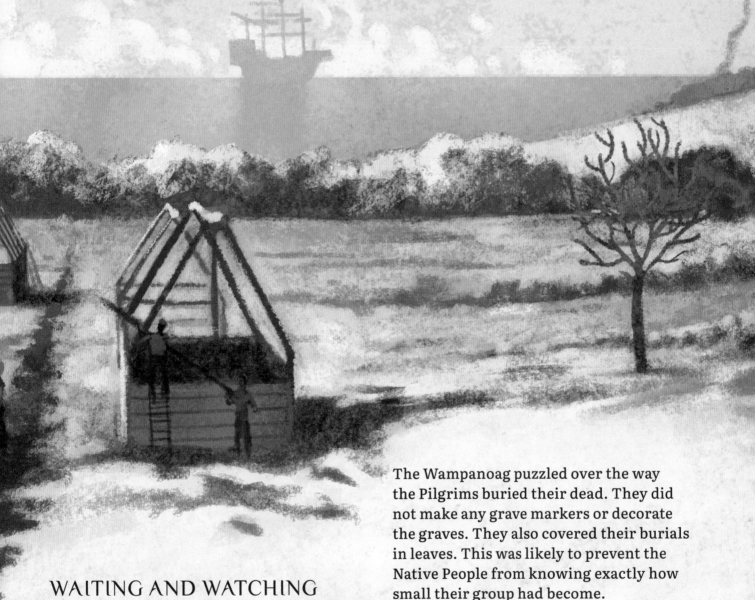

WAITING AND WATCHING

Sometimes, the Pilgrims spotted smoke in the distance. It came from Wampanoag fires—a reminder that they were not alone in New Plymouth. The Wampanoag kept their distance and watched as these strange new settlers struggled with their land.

The Wampanoag puzzled over the way the Pilgrims buried their dead. They did not make any grave markers or decorate the graves. They also covered their burials in leaves. This was likely to prevent the Native People from knowing exactly how small their group had become.

In truth, the Pilgrims' number was frightfully small. What had begun as a group of over 100 had fallen to just 53. The *Mayflower*'s crew had also shrunk. About half of them died during that long, terrible winter.

47

BRINGING THE CANNONS

Finally, spring arrived. The small, weak group of Pilgrims worked to build their new settlement. Those who were strong enough began planting gardens. Others cut down trees and shaped the wood for homebuilding. Some explored the area for fishing and hunting. The Pilgrims laid out the plans for a small neighborhood. They decided that each family was to build its own home.

STOLEN TOOLS

One day, Myles Standish and another Pilgrim were cutting down trees a short distance from the settlement. They took a break to eat lunch, but when they returned to their work, they discovered that their tools had been stolen. The thieves, the Pilgrims knew, had been the Native People. This left them feeling rattled. If the Native People were bold enough to steal from them, then they might be ready to attack. The Pilgrims hurried to make New Plymouth ready for battle. The settlers made sure their guns were clean and ready to shoot. They elected Standish as their military captain.

A CONFUSING INTERACTION

While the Pilgrims were discussing the best way to defend their community, two figures appeared on a nearby hillside. They were Native People. They gestured to the Pilgrims. The Pilgrims gestured back and approached them. Suddenly, a great noise arose from the woods behind the two native men. It sounded like a large group of people. Just then, the two men on the hillside darted off into the woods. It was a confusing and surprising moment.

The Pilgrims responded by removing some of the cannons from the *Mayflower* and hauling them up a nearby hill. This took time and energy, slowing down the progress they had been making on their homes. However, it also made the settlement at New Plymouth feel safer. Pilgrims standing behind the cannons could see much of the surrounding forests and harbor. Anyone who tried to attack them would face a fiery fight.

MEETING THE NATIVE PEOPLE

One spring day, the Pilgrims were surprised to see a Native man walk quietly into their settlement. Adding to their shock the man greeted them in English: "Welcome, Englishmen."

PATUXET

The Pilgrims soon learned that their visitor was Samoset. Samoset was a sagamore, or leader, of the Abenaki people. He had learned English from trading with European fishermen. He told them that New Plymouth used to be a village called Patuxet, but it was now empty because a terrible disease had killed most of the area's people.

Samoset told them more about the Native People in the area. The Pilgrims still called them savages, but they were actually a group of Wampanoag called the Pokanoket. They were led by a sachem named Ousamequin, meaning "Yellow Feather," whom the Pilgrims would call Massasoit. To the south of New Plymouth was a group of Wampanoag allies called the Nauset. Samoset warned the Pilgrims that the Nauset were angry with them. The stolen corn had belonged to them. Samoset told the Pilgrims that it had been the Nauset who had attacked them at First Encounter. It had also been the Nauset who had stolen the Pilgrims' building tools.

Samoset became an important figure to the Pilgrims. He introduced them to some Pokanoket people, including a man they called Tisquantum. Tisquantum was from Patuxet. He had survived the plague there only because he had been kidnapped by English sailors before it happened. His kidnappers took him to Europe, where he learned English. Now he was back in America with Massasoit.

Tisquantum told the Pilgrims Massasoit was close by. Soon, the great leader emerged from a nearby hillside. He was an impressive figure. Sixty men followed in a grand train.

PEACE TREATY

The Pilgrims invited Massasoit and some of his men into one of their new buildings. Tisquantum translated and both sides agreed to a peace treaty. The Pilgrims declared that neither group would steal from or harm one another. Also, they would not ally with either side's enemies, or bring weapons into their meetings. Finally, the Pilgrims declared that Massasoit and his men would become the friends and allies of King James.

Massasoit was a shrewd leader. Though the Pilgrims were weak, he was eager to become their allies. The Wampanoag were at war with a tribe called the Narragansett. The Narragansett traded heavily with Europeans. Massasoit probably thought that partnering with the Pilgrims would make the Narragansett less likely to attack, as they would not want to anger their trading partners.

This agreement marked the official start of a partnership. The Wampanoag and the Pilgrims would try to work together.

LEARNING TO LIVE

On April 5, most of the *Mayflower*'s remaining crew returned to the ship, lifted anchor, and set sail for England. These men had not intended to stay in America. The *Mayflower* voyage had simply been work for them. However, five crewmembers remained with the Pilgrims. These sailors had either been hired to help grow the settlement during its first year, or had decided to become colonists themselves.

Tisquantum also stayed in Plymouth to help the Pilgrims. He showed them where to forage for food and taught them about the "three sisters"—a way of growing corn with squash and beans, so the plants work together. The bean plants climb the tall corn stalks, and the broad squash leaves block sunlight to prevent weeds from growing.

With Tisquantum's help, the Pilgrims were able to produce enough food for themselves. By midsummer, they were able to repay the Nauset for their stolen corn. Finally, their little settlement began to prosper.

THE FIRST THANKSGIVING

New Plymouth was filled with the sound of chatter, laughter, and clanking metal plates. It was the fall of 1621, and the Pilgrims had much to celebrate.

Thanks to Tisquantum, the Pilgrims had enough food to survive. Their little settlement now had seven homes and four storage buildings. The Pilgrims had also extended their friendships to other groups of Native People. On September 13, 1621, Pilgrim leaders signed a peace treaty with nine Native leaders. This was a great relief to the Pilgrims, who had arrived in New England with many fears about its inhabitants.

CELEBRATION

As the Pilgrims collected their first harvest, they were overcome with appreciation. They had managed to grow twenty acres of corn, and six acres of barley and peas. To celebrate, some men went out to shoot fowl for a feast. Their musket shots boomed in the woodland. In addition to bringing in enough meat to feed the colony for a week, the gunshots also attracted the attention of the Pokanoket. Massasoit showed up at New Plymouth with ninety of his men. The Pilgrims invited their curious guests to stay for a meal.

In addition to the birds shot by the Pilgrims, which may have included turkey, the Pokanoket added five deer. Vegetables, fruits, fish, lobsters, and oysters might have also been eaten. For several days, the ninety Pokanoket and fifty Pilgrims ate, talked, shot one another's weapons, and played games.

Both groups had a strong tradition of giving thanks for their fortunes. The Puritan Pilgrims often said a prayer of thanks before and after each meal. The Pokanoket, too, regularly gave thanks for their food. The Pilgrims did not label this celebration the First Thanksgiving. It was simply a happy event.

MODERN THANKSGIVING

In 1863, president Abraham Lincoln declared Thanksgiving an American national holiday. It would be celebrated on the fourth Thursday of November. This became a celebrated part of American culture.

In 1970, a group of Native People protested this. They declared that Thanksgiving was a "National Day of Mourning." A Wampanoag man named Wamsutta (Frank B.) James wrote that Massasoit's decision to welcome the Pilgrims "was perhaps our biggest mistake. We, the Wampanoag, welcomed you, the white man, with open arms, little knowing that it was the beginning of the end…"

Today, Thanksgiving remains an important American holiday. People celebrate it by spending time with family, giving thanks, and watching sports. However, many Americans also spend this day remembering the impact the Pilgrims had on North America's Native People.

NEW PLYMOUTH GROWS

In the days after their Thanksgiving feast, the Pilgrims spotted something unusual on the water. It was a small ship. They began to panic. It might be a French warship, come to attack. The Pilgrims armed themselves and prepared to fight. Thankfully, the new ship was an English vessel called the *Fortune*. It carried 35 passengers who wanted to join the settlement at New Plymouth.

But as the Pilgrims' fears calmed, the people on board the *Fortune* developed worries of their own. Seeing New Plymouth for the first time was upsetting. It was small and sparse. At one point, the *Fortune*'s passengers even discussed abandoning New Plymouth altogether. The ship's captain had to talk them out of their frenzy. The *Fortune*'s passengers reluctantly trudged ashore.

For their part, the New Plymouth Pilgrims were disappointed to see the new arrivals as well. They had not brought any supplies, and were weak and hungry. Instead of helping New Plymouth, they might simply drain its resources. But the community welcomed its new members anyway. Most of the newcomers were young men, and the Pilgrims knew they could help to build and to farm their new homeland.

In the summer of 1623, two more ships arrived. The *Anne* and the *Little James* brought about 60 more people to the little town. Finally, New Plymouth began to operate successfully. That fall, the settlement produced enough food for all of its people.

CUTTHROATS
The Pilgrims' relationship with the Native People grew tense. Tisquantum was caught trying to overthrow Massasoit. Then rumors circulated that the Native People might attack New Plymouth. To discourage this, Myles Standish led an assault on the Massachusetts people in 1623, killing many. The violent attack earned the Pilgrims a new nickname: Wotawquenange, meaning "cutthroats."

WHAT BECAME OF THE MAYFLOWER?

Journeying to New Plymouth was not the *Mayflower's* last adventure. Captain Christopher Jones sailed her to France and back in the fall of 1621, her cargo hold heavy with bay salt. Jones died the following spring.

Little is known about where the *Mayflower* sailed in the years after Jones's death. In 1624, the ship was very old and in poor condition. She was likely torn apart and her scraps sold or destroyed.

This might have been a sad ending for a ship, but the story of the *Mayflower's* importance was only just beginning. The passengers she had carried across the ocean four years earlier were busy building a community that would, just 152 years later, become the United States of America. Their descendants would always remember the vessel that had helped birth a nation: a little ship called the *Mayflower*.

THE NATIVE PEOPLE

The stories of the Native People did not end when the Pilgrims began to prosper. Samoset continued to live and interact with European settlers, and likely supervised the first land sale to them. Tisquantum remained an important guide and interpreter for the Pilgrims. He died in 1622. Massasoit led the Pokanoket Wampanoag until his death in 1660. His son, Metacom (also called King Philip) led a violent uprising against the English in a conflict known as King Philip's War.

TIMELINE

NOVEMBER 9, 1620
People on the *Mayflower* spot Cape Cod.

A group of Scrooby separatists attempts to leave England, but are arrested.

JULY, 1620
The separatists travel to Delfthaven. There, they board the *Speedwell* and sail to Southampton, where they meet the *Mayflower*.

An English sailor named Thomas Hunt kidnaps a group of Patuxet and Nauset native people and tries to sell them into slavery in Europe. Tisquantum is one of his captives.

AUGUST 21, 1620
Both ships set sail again, but problems on the *Speedwell* force them to harbor in Plymouth, England.

DECEMBER 8, 1620
The Nauset people and the Pilgrims exchange fire in the First Encounter.

1607	1608	1614	1616-1619	1620

A terrible disease sweeps through the Wampanoag, causing up to 90% of their people to die. The Wampanoag call it "the Great Dying."

SEPTEMBER 6, 1620
The *Mayflower* departs from Plymouth, England.

The separatists successfully flee to Holland.

AUGUST 5, 1620
The *Speedwell* and *Mayflower* set sail for America, but the *Speedwell* soon develops a leak. The boats return to England.

NOVEMBER 11, 1620
The *Mayflower* drops anchor inside Cape Cod Bay, now known as Provincetown Harbor.

DECEMBER 16, 1620
The *Mayflower* drops anchor in New Plymouth Harbor.

WINTER 1620–1621
Half of the passengers and crew die from disease.

APRIL 5, 1621
The *Mayflower* sets sail for England.

MARCH 16, 1621
Samoset enters New Plymouth and introduces himself.

NOVEMBER 9, 1621
The *Fortune* arrives in New Plymouth, bringing 35 Pilgrims.

President Abraham Lincoln declares Thanksgiving to be a national holiday.

1621	1623	1863	1970

MARCH 22, 1621
Tisquantum enters New Plymouth and introduces the Pilgrims to Massasoit. Massasoit signs a peace treaty with the Pilgrims.

SEPTEMBER 13, 1621
Nine more Native leaders sign a peace treaty with the Pilgrims that states they are "the loyal subjects of King James, king of Great Britain."

JULY AND AUGUST, 1623
The *Anne* and *Little James* arrive in New Plymouth. Together, the ships bring about 100 new Pilgrims.

DECEMBER 20, 1620
The Pilgrims decide to settle in the abandoned Patuxet village. They call it New Plymouth.

FALL, 1621
The Pilgrims and Pokanoket feast together in celebration of the Pilgrim's first harvest. This would later become known as the First Thanksgiving.

A group of Native People declare Thanksgiving a national day of mourning.

AUTHOR'S NOTE

Rebecca Siegel wrote this book with an odd stack of papers piled next to her computer. Grown faint from years of careful hands, they record in detail her husband's family lineage. Photocopied pages from tattered old bibles show lists of names in neat, looping script. Old family trees connect one family to another, linking the past to the present. At the bottom of the stack were three faded photographs. Two showed a boxy, weather-worn house with a red front door. The other showed a white wooden sign, reading "Howland House."

Siegel's husband is a descendant of John Howland, the *Mayflower* passenger who had the bad luck of falling off the ship, and the good fortune to be hauled back aboard. These papers trace 14 generations of his family. But more than that, they show how a country has changed over time. John Howland came to New England because he wanted religious freedom. It is little wonder, then, that his descendant would reflect that. The Siegel family tree has proud Jewish, Catholic, and Protestant branches.

Writing this book was a great adventure for Siegel. In addition to combing through old family resources, she also did her best to read everything she could from the original travelers themselves. This included letters sent from the Pilgrims to investors back home, pamphlets printed by the Pilgrims while still in Leiden,

and texts such as *Mourt's Relation* and *History of Plymouth Plantation, 1620-1647*.

But Siegel didn't just want to tell one side of the story. She was deeply committed to telling the Pokanoket side as well. Understanding that her perspective would be skewed by her non-Native background, Siegel collaborated with Wampanoag people, including Chief George Spring Buffalo of the Pocassett Wampanoag Tribe of the Pokanoket Nation, to ensure that the language and imagery in this book was accurate and appropriate.

When learning about the *Mayflower* and its passengers, Siegel encourages readers to look for Wampanoag-authored histories as well. Doing so will help to paint a fuller picture of this crucial moment in North American history.

MODERN DESCENDANTS

Today, there are about 35 million living descendants of the *Mayflower* passengers. Ten million of these live in America. Some are very famous. Others are ordinary people with an extraordinary lineage. You might have a relative who sailed on this voyage, or who was among the Pokanoket who met these Pilgrims. Do some research online or at your local library to find out. You might make an interesting discovery!

PRESIDENTS

Eight American presidents, including John Adams, John Quincy Adams, Zachary Taylor, Ulysses S. Grant, James Garfield, Franklin Delano Roosevelt, George H.W. Bush, George W. Bush, and Calvin Coolidge, can trace their lineage back to the *Mayflower*.

JULIA CHILD (1912-2004), a famous chef and television personality, was a descendant of William Brewster.

Model and actor MARILYN MONROE (1926-1962) was a descendant of John Alden.

Actor ALEC BALDWIN (born 1958) is a descendant of John Howland.

Astronaut ALAN SHEPARD (1923-1998) was a descendant of passenger Richard Warren.

NATIVE PEOPLE

Disease, famine, violence, and oppression killed most of the Wampanoag who lived near the settlement at New Plymouth. But, not all. As one modern Wampanoag woman told the author of this book, American children need to understand one important thing: "What they need to know is that we survived."

CHARD BRITTERIDGE ∗ PETER BROWNE ∗ EDMUND MARGESSON ∗ GILBERT WINSLOW ∗ THOMAS WILLIAMS ∗
LIZABETH TILLEY ∗ JOAN HURST TILLEY ∗ JOHN TILLEY ∗ HUMILITY COOPER ∗ HENRY SAMPSON ∗ ANN TILLEY ∗
LERTON ∗ MARY NORRIS ALLERTON ∗ ISAAC ALLERTON ∗ MARY MORE ∗ RICHARD MORE ∗ WRESTLING BREWSTER

63

INDEX

FIND OUT MORE

Learn more about the *Mayflower's* voyage and the birth of a nation with the books and websites below.

Books:

Arenstam, Peter et al. *Mayflower 1620: A New Look at a Pilgrim Voyage.* Washington, DC: National Geographic Children's Books, 2007.

Cunningham, Kevin and Peter Benoit. *The Wampanoag.* New York: Scholastic, 2011.

O'Neil Grace, Catherine. *1621: A New Look at Thanksgiving.* Washington, DC: National Geographic, 2004.

Websites:

http://mayflowerhistory.com
https://www.plimoth.org/learn/just-kids